CHOSEN DAUGHTERS

You Were Never Fatherless

CARMEN S. McLEAN

Write Way Publishing
Company LLC

Chosen Daughters You Were Never Fatherless

Copyright © 2017 Carmen S. McLean

Printed in the United States of America
ISBN 978-1-946425-05-8

Book design by CSinclaire Write-Design
Cover design by DGuevara Traffic Peddlers
Cover image by Jarvis Peacock

Write Way Publishing
Company LLC

CHOSEN DAUGHTERS

You Were Never Fatherless

Dedication

To my Father and only Father who chose me for such a time as this: Thanks for being my first love. Thank you for loving me in a beautiful way. Thank you for watching over me when I was lost. Thank you for giving me another chance to live life. I have walked out on you so many times, and you patiently waited with open arms until I returned. I can honestly feel the love you have for me. I will never leave you again. You are my joy, my strength, and my peace.

To my mother, Lilly: Thank you for never giving up. I don't think you know how much strength I have pulled from you. Thank you for keeping me covered in your prayers. Thank you for always standing in the gap between my daughter and me. You have kept us together through the good times and the bad. Last, but not least, thank you for teaching me how to have trust in my Father.

To my daughter, Robin: You are the daughter God chose for me. You are a gifted, beautiful, unique little woman who doesn't know her full potential yet. It was you who pushed me past my fears. You were there to cheer me on when I was stepping out of my comfort zone and learning to become a woman. You were there to experience the highs and the lows with me. I am proud to see that you are learning to manage your pain and press past your sorrows. My prayer for you today and forever is that God continues to reveal to you who He is and who you are in Him. I pray you know He has already chosen you to be His daughter.

Acknowledgments

Willa Mae Thompson

Thank you so much for supporting me in life. You have shown and taught me things that have helped make me the woman I am now. You cared for me like I was your daughter. Please know that you will always have a special place in my heart. I love you more than you will ever know.

Sarah Senter

Thank you so much for your support. You are someone I truly can trust and rely on for help. Thank you for helping to make my dreams come true.

Preface

How can we live in this world and yet not know our Heavenly Father is watching over us the whole time?

During my journey, I have noticed the actions of women who didn't have fathers present in their lives. They travel through their lives hoping and wishing they had someone to care for them and make them feel complete.

In general, as women, we think we need validation from people. And if we don't receive it, life has no meaning to us. We tend to compensate by trying to force people to fit into our boxes, or we make them create room for us in their lives. We even do this when others really don't have the tools or capacity to love us the way we should be loved. Neither do they have an understanding of who we are.

But a bigger concern is do *you* know who *you* are? Do you know who created you? Do you know why He chose you to be His daughter? Do you know where you are going—or why He set you apart for your journey?

Before we go any further, I want you to ask God to let you hear Him say, "I knew you before you were formed in your mother's womb." Ask Him to speak these words over you while you are awake and while you are asleep.

He created and chose you to be His daughter before you were even born! The most important part is that He meets you right where you are. He is prepared to help you through your unanswered questions as a fatherless daughter and to guide you to His path of peace.

I share many things about myself on the following pages. Don't worry, my heart is already healed. My Father has accepted me as His daughter. My goal is to help you heal from pain and hurt that weren't supposed to be there— to release the fears, insecurities, and limitations given to you by people you thought you knew and that you loved. He wanted your path clear from the beginning, but it is okay; He has a solution. He always does.

Open your mind to receive Him, open your heart to love Him, and open your lips to praise Him. He can only reveal Himself to you as your Father if you are ready for this journey. Start as soon as you can!

Table of Contents

Introduction

Where Did You Come From and Where Are You Going?

Traveling started early for me as a child growing up. I went from North Carolina to New York every summer and holiday. Seems like every time I turned around, I was back on a plane again. My father, his wife, and his stepson lived in New York. I couldn't quite understand at the time why I was going back and forth, but it was out of my control at age seven. My mother didn't explain what type of man my father was. It was left up to me to find out what purpose he had in my life. She kept it classy and never spoke badly about him or the situation. I admire her to this day for that. At that time, I probably would not have believed any negative stories anyway.

The summer days and holidays were uncomfortable for me. At night, I could always hear them arguing over why I got more than my stepbrother. I would spend time with my dad but then come home not knowing why I had been there. I thought it was strange, but I wanted to see if things would change as I got older. They didn't. I continued to see him just because I was told to by my mother. I never had a chance to know him as a father or to express my love for him because I was always competing with his new family.

And he was okay with letting them win. My father finally stopped sending for me when he had to make the decision to choose between them and me. I had no anger, felt no void, nor held any bitterness toward him at the time. I adjusted to the waves and moved on with just living with my mother and six brothers.

My mother was the heroine in the house. She disciplined us and loved us at the same time. She was a strong woman for that. I would have been lost without her. My brothers took on the responsibility of raising and guiding me. I knew they meant well, but there was still something missing. I felt I needed something stronger in my life. I began searching for the man who would love me inside and out. He would love the little girl in me and the woman I was becoming. I could do no wrong in his eyes. But it would only be right if this unconditional love came from my father first—the strong man I thought would be my first love. The one I would return to when I bumped my head a thousand times and cried so profusely he would hold me until I stopped. The one who would one day tell me about how a man should treat a woman.

I thought, as a daughter, I was entitled to all of this. I soon realized it wasn't going to happen for me. So,

I grew up quickly only to run into walls and people who hurt and abused me. I didn't connect that the void from not having a father in my life was the reason why I was going astray. My behavior was out of control, and I was creating more and more drama for myself. For years, I struggled with conflict. I was drawn to broken people.

The warning lights were going off everywhere, and I still kept going in that direction. I had no discernment to let me know my left from my right, and the people I was around didn't have any clues either. I was in situations that could have placed me at a crime scene or led me to my death. As I look back, I wasted so many opportunities to grow as a woman. I gave so much of myself to people who were never meant to come into contact with my spirit. The little girl in me was just afraid to get it together. And definitely I felt I had no hope to see anything different in my life. But somewhere, deep down inside, I knew I was still being watched over and guided. I wondered why that was. Now I know.

He Has Answers for Us if We Listen

Luke 1:45 — "Blessed is she who believes that the lord would fulfill His promises to her."

Can you recall looking over your life wondering how you made it out of certain situations? Do you know why you were removed from certain people? Do you know why you heard a small voice in your head that told you to keep going? You didn't even know why you kept going, but you did. It was because you were not alone. God was pushing you closer to Him every step of the way.

The hand you were dealt is no surprise to Him. He will heal you from the difficult things. From the moment you were born, He was guiding and shielding you from danger. He was there blocking all the enemy plans that could have led you to death. Your Father was speaking great words in your ear, telling you which way to move and how far to go. Perhaps you didn't think it was Him, but He was there speaking to you. You thought you were in control of your life the whole time—how silly was that? He takes care of you even when you don't ask Him to. He is the One who prepares you to live in this world.

God wants to ask you two questions: Where have you been? Where are you going? He asked Hagar these questions when she was under the tree. She had no idea, but He had all the answers waiting for her. He just wanted to get her to a place where she was finally desperate for the right answer, a place where He could talk to her One-on-one. God doesn't want us to be confused in this world or be lost from Him. He sees and hears everything. Your Father cares for you in such a way that He finds you even when you don't want to be found. If you are reading this book, these two questions are for you. This is a chance to get to know your Father. The One who has been there the whole time. Yes, the One who called you to be His daughter in the first place.

As you read each chapter, I invite you to reflect on your relationship with your Father. There are questions to help you do this. Think about them and answer them in total honesty. This will help you understand your journey with Him.

Chapter 1

You Have Encircled This Mountain Long Enough

Deuteronomy 2:3 — "You have encircled this mountain long enough."

How Long Will You Keep Circling?

Lord, this week, this month, this year, I truly will make a big change. I will leave my old thinking and take the high road. I will not revert to my past. This is the year for you and me, God. I will stand firm in Your word. I will not go back to an empty heart. My goal will be not to please man but to please you.

I could give you hundreds of sayings like this, but I could not hold fast to any of them.

I started many things in my own strength, only to fail. I didn't seem to take my projects seriously, so I procrastinated. It was hard for me to do things alone. I wanted everyone's help. I felt everyone should be involved in whatever my plan was.

Have you noticed that everyone's path is not the same as your path? God gave you the vision. Waiting on the approval and excitement of others should not be on your list to move forward with the plan. You will be well on your way to unhappiness if you wait for them.

Let me tell you more bad habits that had me encircling the same mountain. I know you can relate to this one. *Lord, please don't let any unwholesome talk come out of my mouth, but only let out what is helpful for building up others.* I truly believe my intentions started out right with every new day, but as the day continued, I would lose my direction. I didn't know how to set boundaries for myself. I still wanted to be part of the conversations in the world. Basically, I wanted to put in my two cents. Deep down inside, I knew I should keep my mouth shut. I should have remembered the others in those conversations may not have been asking God to speak only wholesome, helpful words.

Here goes another one. *Wait! Did I just run into him again? Lord, are you trying to tell me something?* In my loneliness, I told myself it might work this time. Maybe he changed and turned his life over to Christ. I made excuses for him or at least kept trying to give him the benefit of the doubt. But if it hadn't worked before, why would it work now? I had already told him

I was in church and there were certain things I didn't believe in.

Well, he hadn't changed, and I wasted months when I knew it wasn't going to work in the first place. Again, I had created another mountain to go around. And again, I was left with the same pain as before.

The decisions I made in these examples were the root of my problem, but I had no clue how to change what I was doing. The problem ran deeper and stronger than I realized.

Most times, I placed the blame on someone else or on my upbringing. I continued to ask myself why I was falling for things I couldn't get myself out of. Why was I this crazy to allow myself to get hurt over and over? The ups and downs of emotional reactions were draining. I was excited one day and broken the next. From all of this, my immaturity showed up in the relationship and on the job. I wasn't able to express my frustration and anger to anyone else because I did not understand the conflict within myself. Inside I was begging for someone to please help me understand how to figure out life. I knew my poor decisions led me only to suffering.

* * *

You may notice that you are doing the same thing I was. If so, it is time to evaluate why you keep going around the same mountain. Think about the following questions and write your honest answers. These are "Awareness Questions." They will help you move one step closer to becoming whole.

• Awareness Questions •

Why do I keep going back to what feels familiar but always brings bad results?

Do I understand what this does to my life?

What am I afraid of?

Sisters, you can't start the next chapter of your life until you say NO to your negative past. I want us to be on this journey together. You have the power to take the necessary steps to see the new woman you can become. It will require you to think harder and longer about decisions that can affect your integrity and the relationship you want to have with God. Don't lie to yourself, be completely honest. Know what you can do and know what you can't do and still walk with God.

For example, if certain people will take you backwards, slowly remove yourself from them until you can stand firm in your beliefs. If you tend to make certain excuses that prevent you from going in the right direction, plan ahead to have an answer in place to challenge each excuse so you won't fall for it. Remember, your bad habits do not own you. They only have power when you agree to them. I challenge you to become one step closer to the new you every day. You will be rewarded with a new and better you and a new and better life.

God longs to bring you out of confusion. God can make your path straight. If you continue to go around the same mountain again and again, what are you learning? How have you pushed toward the place God is calling you to? Ask yourself if you can trust Him, if you want to follow Him, if you even want to hear from Him. And ask yourself if you can handle the corrections God is going to give you. Yes, it will be frightening and things will start to shift, but they will shift only for the better.

Your Father is giving you what you have deserved from the beginning. Sometimes your mind might not be prepared for what lies ahead. But now is the right time to start going in the direction you were meant to go. We all are used to lowering our standards and not waiting for the people God sends us to share our lives with. God has chosen His daughters to love more, want more, and create more. He wants you to walk with your head held high. He wants you to have healthy relationships with people who truly care about the inner you.

The Holy Spirit is there to help you do the right things. You should try using Him. His Spirit is the one thing that will lead you to His truth. Don't allow the world to be your teacher rather than the One who loves you. Your Father is here to teach you, not punish you. Seek Him first; He will give you His truth. He knows your hidden issues, and He has answers to your deepest questions. Even ones you can't always articulate to Him or anyone else.

I want to share with you, chosen daughters, that life is too short for you to go around the same mountain for months or years. You must learn to be disciplined and take heed of your negative experiences. Your Father is waiting for you to be strong and bold in His word. And the sooner you get started, the sooner you will be able to see new results.

Her Prison

2 Corinthians 10:5 — "We destroy arguments and every lofty opinion raised against the knowledge of God and take every thought captive to obey God."

Many times we strive to change our lives so we see things differently than we did in the past. We change our looks, we get new friends, and we move to a new location, all intended to set us in a new direction. We believe all these things will bring us peace and joy. But all of this will only lead us back to our past if we don't uncover our personal truth.

I created this prison cell in my mind that drew me back every night to lie in bed crying for God to change my situation. I wasn't over my past or over the little girl who hurt for so many years. The pain and the hurt had caused me to lock up my mind for years. No matter what new experiences I created, I traveled back to the negative ones. I constantly chastised myself with negative self-talk. *You didn't go to a four-year college. You didn't come from an honored family. You are not smart enough to have that man you want. No good thing will come out of you.*

Those things ran through my mind constantly. I repeated the same behaviors I learned growing up. I wouldn't allow myself to see better days ahead of me. So I continued to be stuck in the same vicious cycle passed down from generation to generation. I entered into situations blindfolded, made decisions out of fear and hurt, was controlled and manipulated into loss of identity, and neglected to love myself. I was limiting my ability to understand all the things my Father placed inside of me. Things like He created me in His image. He died for my sins. And my steps are ordered by the Lord.

What prison are you creating for yourself? What cycles are you creating or still continuing?

We think we have all the answers. We carry the burden when it is not even our burden. We deplete ourselves for people who are not supposed to be in our lives. We fail to take actions to change our learned behaviors. We feel a void. No one can fix that void, sis, but your Father.

God gives you strength to break through the strongholds that have been placed in your life. He is willing to give you new ways and new thoughts so that you can have a better future. Jeremiah 33:3 says, "Call to me and I will answer you and tell you great things, unsearchable things you do not know." How amazing is that! He already has an answer set in place for you whenever you are ready to move forward. You don't have to hang on to what has happened to you or what someone has taught you that doesn't add up with what God has spoken over your life.

Are you aware that you are a daughter of the High Priest? Accept this and you can release past mistakes and failures that you have placed on yourself.

I'm confessing to you that I tried everything before I met God. I thought new faces were going to bring me new happiness. I thought new cities were going to break my cycles. None of these new things healed my heart or took me away from my past. I was still stuck in that same dark cell in my mind. I had to open up my heart to my Father. God had to release me from my prison. He had to remove the marks that were created in my mind. I had to let go of everything that was stopping me from living the abundant life that God wanted for me.

Was I scared? Of course! I didn't want to cope with my past or even face it. I was afraid of change. If this sounds familiar to you, just know with the help of God, you can overcome the enemy's plan, which is to have you see things as if they aren't going to change. Do not give the enemy that satisfaction.

The devil tells you the same old, tired stories every day. Don't you want to hear something new? Your Father has been creating new things since the beginning of this world. In Isaiah 43:19 He tells you, "See I am doing a new thing! Now it springs up; do you not perceive it? I am making a way in the wilderness and streams in the wasteland." With those words spoken over your life, He can bring change to you at any moment.

You have a choice: remain stuck in prison or free yourself with the love God has for you. It is just that simple. My advice to you is to ask God to show you the truth. Keep your eyes focused on Him so that He can make you stronger. I dare you to challenge Him to make you new. You will not regret your decision. Go for the gusto. Break out of prison. And bring other sisters out with you.

Chapter 2

Set Apart

1 Peter 2:9 — "But you are not like that, for you are a chosen people. You are royal priests, a holy nation, God's very own possession..."

God is searching the earth for daughters who are ready to serve Him boldly. He needs you to know that you are in the world but not a part of the world. You are going to have to be strong to tell the world, "You no longer own me. God is my master."

May I share with you what being set apart means to me? To me, being set apart means to be the salt of the world. It means to come out from the world and become more like Jesus. When you become set apart, no longer are you answering to people or your flesh. You are calling on God to help you become righteous and holy for Him. In other words, you are giving God the glory to use you to advance His kingdom.

For many years, I still bumped my head and stuck my

hands into things I should have left alone. I knew God had called me from certain places and things. I got lonely and caught myself chasing things that weren't leading me closer to Him. The relationships I tried to force were ending in ugly turmoil. I compromised on behaviors that were well below the standards I put in place for myself. Many times I justified the way I acted in the moment. My heart wanted to be with God, but my mind was pleasing the world. I began to be dissatisfied in every area of my life. Literally, it felt like I was battling even the air. I wanted the anointing, but I didn't want to leave behind the craziness.

A Little Secret

God separates us to save us!

But God is a faithful God. He gave me my answer in one scripture that set me straight. 2 Corinthians 6:14 says, "Do not be joined together with those who do not belong to Christ. How can that which is good get along with that which is bad? How can light be in the same space with darkness?" This scripture brought me clarity from my confusion. Those words have so much power in them. And I chose to obey His word.

My passion is for God to use me to help women see themselves in a better light. I recall asking God to separate me from anything that was not pleasing to Him.

I wanted Him to separate me so that He could use me to be a light for women who were in darkness. I knew He gave me a desire to influence women. But how could I be a light to someone else if I was still bringing darkness to my situation? I did not want to be a stumbling block. I wanted Him to use me as a building block to help others.

You may think the worst thing that someone can do to you is to remove you from things that you have been attached to for a long time. Your Father has been separating you from others your whole life. He has been getting you prepared to serve Him. Everything He does is intentional. The twists and turns He has given you are for His purposes. He is the force behind every situation to get you right where He needs you. He is teaching you life lessons that will only benefit you. Proverbs 3:5 says, "Trust in the lord with all your heart and lean not on your own understanding."

It is hard to be separated from familiar things, places, and people. You may not understand, at the time, why God pushes and pulls you away from certain things, places, or even people. You may get frustrated and lonely, not thinking that God has something or someone better for you or someplace better for you to go.

Are you struggling with this situation? Are you trying to serve two masters? Are you allowing yourself to answer the way the world does? Is that man in your life leading you to Christ? Are you afraid of being alone for a season?

When God calls you away from things that are no longer or never have been pleasing to Him and leads you toward Him, you have to believe that He is up to something good for you. Always hold on to that in your spirit. He is ready to make you part of Him. And when He allows you to become part of Him, He has to cut away dead things first. Your flesh wants to go back to gossiping, cursing out people, or hanging at the club. I am here to tell you that you can't answer to God and to the devil at the same time. One is going to go unanswered. And believe me, you don't want it to be God.

Satan knows your weaknesses and your downfalls. The enemy is waiting for you to fall back in the same traps. He plots to abuse or destroy you completely. But God will change your whole position before He allows Satan to win. I remember God uprooting me from a place so that the enemy would stop tormenting me. I was hired to become a store manager in another city. I thought it was the best thing God had done for me in my life. It was right around time I thought I couldn't take anymore. I thought I was left for dead. But God had another way out for me. I was in a situation that was not good for me. With the new opportunity, God moved me away from the danger I was encountering where I was.

Can I say He is an on-time God? As a daughter of God, you have to trust that He acts in your best interest. We all allow ourselves to waste time on things that don't transform us to think better or be better. Your Father wants His children to be living examples. He knows sometimes you will stumble in life. He doesn't expect perfection. But you must keep following Him to know His perfect ways. You can no longer afford to walk with Satan.

The enemy has confused you for so many years. The enemy entices you to play on his playground. He wants you to believe that you can play with him and still receive God's full glory. He tries to convince you that he can give you things. James 1:17 says, "Every good and perfect gift is from above, and comes down from the Father of heavenly light, who does not change like shifting shadows."

Why would you open doors that will have you back in confusion and fear? Why would you even allow the enemy to play with your mind? His number one goal is to separate you from the One who knows you by name. The devil doesn't care to know you or your name. He cares about how many souls he can separate from God. You must be careful not cross over into Satan's territories.

Please do not underestimate his power. Satan has studied your past patterns. He is here to take your soul in exchange for nothing. I have learned that the enemy plays the same tricks over and over with God's daughters. But you must know that God has already won the victory.

Being set apart is amazing! God can use us to change the next generation if we let Him. He has chosen us to live a life that will allow us to produce good fruit. He withholds no good thing from those who walk uprightly. He is ready to give us authority and power.

Your family and friends are waiting to be delivered from bondage and limitations because you made the decision to stand with God. Can you imagine helping God change laws, ministering to people, or maybe even writing songs that will influence people's lives? Did you forget that He is the Creator of Heaven and Earth? Ask yourself these questions: *Why did He separate me? Why did He allow me to go through painful things?* He has a reason!

* * *

I encourage you to see what God has in store for you. Let God blow your mind! Think about these questions and record your heartfelt answers.

• Awareness Questions •

How are you showing others that you live under God's rule?

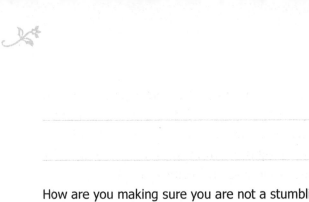

How are you making sure you are not a stumbling block to others?

How do you renew your mind daily to support being set apart?

Describe how you think God has set you apart.

_____

_____

_____

_____

_____

Chapter 3

Thorns in Her Garden

Philippians 4:6 — "Do not be anxious about anything..."

Slow Down, Don't Be Anxious

I admit it! There are days I still get anxious about my life. I start to play the game, the "what ifs." For example, what if I was married? What if I had a father? What if I lived in a two-parent home? What if I had more kids or no kids? What if I don't get the degree? I can give a million "what ifs," but, in truth, they are neither here nor there.

My emotional state of mind used to take me on many roller coaster rides. Some days I found myself getting irritable at people because I felt inadequate or broken. My relationships with men didn't last long, and it was always "their fault." I wanted to rush and see the ending before I even knew him, treating every man as if he were my husband. I wanted to control everything that happened in my life.

Wow! I was so wrong on so many levels for that one. In other areas of my life, I also hurried to make decisions. I would start a business or take a class. I thought this would bring me pleasure. My thoughts were "it won't hurt to try it." I felt that I always would be stuck at my job, that I always would be single, and that I would never discover my purpose if I somehow did not move forward.

The more I tried to do new things that were not a part of God's plan, the more frustrated I became with life. Sometimes I got so desperate that I started to look for signs from every direction. I couldn't quite figure out why some people "made it" but I was still at the starting line. It would have been nice to feel some sense of accomplishment.

I began to think that maybe my life was difficult but no one else's was. I felt that not having a father took so many advantages from me. Oh yeah, the excuses came from far and wide. I felt time was not on my side. Have you ever felt that way?

Guess what? We all are anxious about something in life. We all have pondered on the "what ifs." I know right now you are thinking, "What can I do about my situation? What else do I need to accomplish to satisfy this person or myself?" I want you start examining what's driving you to be anxious. Whatever it is, take time and decide if you need it or if it is just something to feed your flesh.

I wouldn't be nice if I didn't tell you about my special friends patience and trust. They will be helpful guides for your walk with God. It is no surprise to God how many requests we give Him or questions we ask Him because we don't see the full picture. We ask Him, "Father, do you know everyone else around me is winning? Father, did you see that ring on her finger? Father, did you notice she got promoted again?" We rush to God to fix or complete things that might not be in His plan for us.

I know I go back and forth with God asking for things that I am not yet prepared to receive. I have learned that my Father knows what is best for me. Believe me, you are not missing out on anything! He sees the hidden things behind the doors. He understands which people will be in your life for only a season. God's path is comprehensive. Trust that in each situation He gives you, He is allowing you to grow and become healthy. He has the right timing for you to shine bright like a diamond. He's not worried about the "what ifs." He cares about preparing you to be a great daughter for Him.

It is truly up to you to get rid of the "what ifs." Life is moving along every day whether we move forward or we get stuck in the "what ifs." I know I can't go back and change things, but I can see things in a new way. You shouldn't rush just to go nowhere, especially if God's hand is not on the situation. Maybe it is not the right time or season for what God has in mind for you. It takes discernment and wisdom to learn what you need in that time He has set for you.

Discontentment stirs up the heart and confuses the mind. It will cause you to question God about what He is doing with you or for you. You must learn to be content with what God chooses to give you. 1 Peter 5:17 says, "Cast all your anxieties on Him, because He cares for you." He doesn't want you to go without or to beg for things that He can give you in a moment. He supplies all your needs. God has been and is faithful to you—past and present. You know He will come through in the future. God definitely wants to see you happy. He receives glory when you accomplish your goals.

No matter what has happened to you in the past, it is time for you to live life on purpose. Eliminate the fear that has set in your life. As you continue to let Him lead your life, He will remind you that He knows exactly where you are.

* * *

When you have decisions to make, ask yourself the following questions.

• Awareness Questions •

Did I ask God what He wants for me?

Have I considered if this is a major decision or a minor
decision?

Am I rushed by fear to make a decision?

Will one direction lead me on God's path better than the other?

I Have So Many Flaws

Psalm 139: 14 — "I am fearfully and wonderfully made; marvelous are thy works; and that my soul knows very well."

There is nothing more heartbreaking than seeing someone you love feel as if they are not beautiful. The world and I could tell my daughter many times that she was beautiful and could be a model, but it was up to her to receive and believe it. She worried about every part of her appearance. The list went on and on. I asked her what flaws she thought she saw because I didn't see them. I reminded her that she was petite and beautiful and that's how God made her. Her image of herself literally stopped her fun and her ability to move forward in life. And all I could do was pray that God would help her see herself through His eyes.

How often do you fight with yourself about the way you see yourself? What lies are you telling yourself about yourself? What is stopping you from choosing the highest thoughts about yourself?

Truth be told, we all will hear negative thoughts in our mind at some time. The thoughts can be about how we look or the struggles we experience or feelings of inadequacies we face. How many times have our feelings about our flaws kept us hostage and from becoming the true person we could be? How many times do we compare ourselves to others? Sometimes we might hesitate to open the business we've been dreaming about, or we stop the application process for school or a new job because we listen to negative self-talk.

The enemy's plan is always to tie up our minds. Satan chooses to intensify the weak parts of us. He doesn't want us to see that we can still move forward or learn to love our flaws. Our minds are powerful, and we cannot allow the one who doesn't own us to gain the advantage in our lives. I have a secret to share with you. We *can* choose to stop the negative self-talk!

I love the Bible story about Moses in Exodus, chapters 3-4. God instructed Moses to lead the Israelites out of Egypt so they could get to the Promised Land. Moses went head-on with the Lord and laid down his flaws immediately when God called him. In Exodus 4:10, Moses said to the Lord, "Pardon your servant, Lord, I have never been eloquent, neither in the past nor since you have spoken to me your servant. I am slow of speech and tongue." Moses went back and forth with the Lord about why he couldn't do what the Lord wanted. "Lord, I am not important enough." "Lord, what shall I say?" " Lord, they will not listen to me."

We give God excuses for things He already knows. This story hits home for a lot of women, including me. We tend to think if we don't have the right upbringing or the right connections, God can't give us a big task. God knows our flaws even before we bring them to Him. He has people set in place to help us live our destiny. God commanded Aaron to go with Moses to speak before the people. How thoughtful was that? He knows the smallest details of our problems. He sees our needs. We have to accept God will help us work through those flaws as we work in His service. Nothing is too hard for our Father. He wants to bring His will to pass; God will get us the help we need.

* * *

• Awareness Questions •

What does God say about flaws?

Do I let my flaws take over my life?

How can I keep moving forward in spite of flaws?

Do I need to see someone to help me get through any weakness?

Guard Your Heart

Proverbs 4:23 — "Above all else guard your heart,
for everything you do flows from it."

As women, we have the tendency to open our hearts
to everything and everybody. Often we don't think

twice before we offer that open heart. We don't consider the impact on others or the others' impact on us. I used to ask God why He gave me a heart so open and why I was so quick to let down my guard. For years I had no boundaries in place to guard my heart. I didn't know how to control my thoughts, and my feelings would be based on how someone else felt that day. I would get hurt easily by things that I knew weren't the truth. People would run in and out of my life, and I kept letting them do it, even when I felt it was not the right thing to do. I handled my heart just like I handled my money. Not very well. They both got away from me without good consequences. These behaviors gave me a bitter heart.

Sisters, we tend to leave God out of the picture when we want what we want. We don't give Him a chance to answer what we need or even to show us who we need in our lives. Sometimes we move too fast and let people into our lives before knowing if they possess the values and morals we should be looking for. We begin to shift our focus to believe what they believe, act how they act. Or we become too wrapped up with what is going on in someone else's life on the Internet; the distraction list can go on and on. Sometimes we don't even know the people we're letting influence us. Every day the world is filling our minds with more distractions. And people and things change all the time in this crazy world. After a while, unwelcome things creep into our hearts and manifest there.

I have learned to block things out of my life. Psalm 119:37 says, "Turn my eyes from worthless things, and give me life through your word." Be aware of what you are letting in your eyes and ears and heart. Be disciplined and self-controlled about what you see and what you listen to. Be just as careful about what you say.

I tell my daughter, Robin, all the time to be intentional about what she looks at on the Internet and social media. It is important to understand each of us is in control of our own heart. The Bible also tells us to stay sober and alert at all times. It's a reminder to stay on guard. Satan's main goal is to get us off the path God is trying to lead us on. God knows all these things we see and hear and feel will form our thoughts and attitudes, and ultimately, they will shape who we are. I know sometimes that we want to be "in the know" or do what everyone else is doing, but God is telling us that is not going to give us peace.

As I grow in my relationship with God, I am becoming more mindful of my thoughts and emotions. I pray daily that I will have the right motives. I pray that God will reveal any hidden or unhidden motives. I believe sometimes we can't hear from God because our hearts are not right. My goal is to hear from God, so I cannot afford to have a sick heart.

Throwing our hearts around like worthless things is not pleasing to God. God expects each of us to have full control over our heart and to watch it carefully. Not your friend. Not your pastor. Not your mother. You are to guard your heart full time. Remember, the heart matters to Him because we serve Him with our hearts. God uses our hearts to help us see Him correctly.

Matthew 5:8 says, "Blessed are the pure in heart, for they shall see God." Don't you want to see God? Don't you want to hear from Him? Keep your heart pure.

From my heart to your heart, please check your heart to make sure it is spiritually healthy. Ask God to continue to examine your heart. Instead of depending on your own understanding, you must seek God's understanding. People cannot give you peace, ONLY GOD CAN GIVE YOU PEACE. And any answer you receive from God will benefit you, not hurt you. I encourage you to spend time with Him to learn what is best for you. Let the Holy Spirit teach you what is healthy for your heart.

* * *

Work through the questions below and write your heartfelt answers.

• Awareness Questions •

Do I put my trust in God or do I put my trust in this world?

_____

_____

Do I cast my cares on God?

Do I allow things of the world to manifest in my heart?

Do I refrain from letting worthless things enter my heart?

God, thank You for teaching us Your truth about guarding our hearts. I pray You change our hearts to become more like Yours. Lord, show up in our hearts so that we may not be far from You. You have a perfect heart. Lord, please remove any impurities and motives from our hearts so that we may see and hear from You more clearly. Increase our awareness to what is pleasing to you so that we can walk in Your way. Holy Spirit, give us a spirit of obedience that we may serve You fully. Please forgive our sins, hidden and unhidden. Establish in us a heart that is sensitive to who You are. Let us rest in knowing that Your thoughts and ways are a better way for us. We pray this in Jesus's name. Amen

Chapter 4

Let God Plant You

Psalm 1:3 — "That person is like a tree planted by streams of water, which yields its fruit in season and whose leaf does not wither—whatever they do prospers."

I remember watching my granny from the window taking care of her garden in the backyard. I was excited to see how she could make her vegetables grow to be beautiful. I could tell back then she was serious about what she planted. She would spend hours prepping and eliminating anything that didn't belong in her garden. Some days during harvest time, I would stand by the door and wait for her to come in with a pile of fresh cucumbers, squash, and tomatoes. Anything she planted, she turned into a delicious meal. Granny let me be the first one to taste anything that came out of her kitchen. I was her assistant in the kitchen. I recall this vividly because these were the special memories that she and I shared.

I know many of God's daughters feel like we were not

planted in the right garden. We weren't watched over or prepared to live life the right way. It almost seems like the day we were born, we were set up for failure. So we decided to plant ourselves without any gardener experience. Our desperate decisions added things to our garden that weren't suppose to live there. We planted anger, fear, low self-esteem, and bitterness all in one section. We watered ourselves daily with hurt and pain. There was no guidance for us on how to produce good fruit. We learned what was needed at the time to help us survive.

Many of us learned how to keep men with our bodies, not our minds. We learned how to manipulate situations just for our own pleasures. Some of us had babies when we were still learning how to love ourselves. Each season had its own problems that made us feel that our garden would never see its full potential.

But we are daughters who don't give up. We raise kids on our own and try to master the life that we see before us. That we do this is powerful, but in reality, we are lost without Father's help.

My decision to let God plant me freed me from every inadequacy that touched my life. He placed me in a new garden. A garden that was full of love and hope. He promised to watch over my garden daily and to water me with His love. My garden has structure and purpose now. I have the opportunity to be nourished well by Him.

No longer am I drifting season to season, finding things to keep me living. He is my living water. I don't need to depend on people to value my worth or teach me their lies. I seek my gardener for His counsel and not my own counsel or the counsel of others. God is there to protect me from things that I can't do in my own strength. That weight is lifted off of me. I can depend on Him to see me through. I am planted in His garden. That means I have a foundation to help me thrive.

If you don't have your foundation to thrive, come and be planted in God's garden.

- In order to grow, we need God's word.

- In order to grow, we need faith.

- In order to grow, we need prayer.

- In order to grow, we need guidance.

God Desires a Relationship with You

When you let God plant you, you are opening the door for your relationship with Him to begin. He desires to fellowship with you and start working in you immediately. You get to see and hear Him first-hand. You can experience how He responds to your situations. You learn His character and how He never changes. You learn what He is capable of doing in your life and the lives of others who are close to you.

To help you grow in the relationship with Him, God provides you with the Holy Spirit to change your heart and teach you His truth. During this time, have faith that He will sustain you now that you are surrendering to Him. We all need His foundation. And most of us want to grow. God is the perfect One to teach us how to do it. His desire is for us to pray to Him, mediate on His word, and listen for His guidance. We don't have to beg Him. He freely gives access to all of Himself to us.

There's no need to struggle or worry at this point. Matthew 6:25-26 says, "Therefore I tell you, do not worry about your life, what you will eat or drink; or about your body, what you will wear. Is not life more than food and the body more than clothes? Look at the birds of the air; they do not sow or reap or store away in barns and yet your heavenly Father feeds them. Are you not much more valuable than they?" I love Him for saying those words to me.

God is so excited to bury your past and bring you into the present. He starts to reveal to you things you couldn't do on your own. Like how to accept the old you while becoming the new you, or how to see things the way He sees them. This is where you can see that He has been waiting for you the whole time, ready to show endless possibilities. Jeremiah 29:11 says, "God plans to prosper you and not harm you, plans to give you hope and future." Do you know what that really means? Sis, you now have a chance to be the true you that was there before you were broken. God has offered you a relationship of a lifetime. He has all the ingredients to make you fruitful. I dare you to accept His offer and give Him your best!

Remember, this will be a process just like any other healthy, growing relationship. It will take time for both of you to understand how to spend time with each other. You may be challenged in new areas, but God is there to cheer you on. He gives you mercy and grace to get this thing right with Him. He cares for you that much. So let go and let God.

* * *

• Awareness Questions •

Am I able to trust God to plant me?

Am I in position for God to plant me?

_____

_____

_____

_____

What do I need for God to plant me?

_____

_____

_____

_____

Chapter 5

A Mother's Love for Her Daughter

2 Timothy 1:5 — "I recall your sincere faith that was alive first in your grandmother Lois and in your mother Eunice, and I am sure is in you."

Mama Prayed Over Me While God Grew Me to Be a Woman

In one ear and out the other. How many times can a mother tell her daughter a hard head makes a soft behind? I think I still hear those words to this day. And yes, my mother still gets on me even in my grown woman years. Seriously, everything she told me to do when I was growing up, I did the opposite. She would tell me to let my hair grow; I would cut it short. She would tell me to wear a dress; I would throw on my pants. She would tell me not to date him; I would love him more.

This wasn't done intentionally to drive her crazy. It was

because I thought I was grown at fifteen. I thought I was making major decisions and controlling my life. The constant arguments going back and forth about "you don't know him, you don't know the situation," or "what can you teach me " were statements always flying under our roof. She was there to protect me from hurt and teach me life's lessons. And I was there to prove her wrong. I didn't want any advice she gave me. Nor did I want her to teach me how to be woman.

How could she give me advice with so many issues and problems I saw her going through that she didn't know how to fix? The men who hurt her and she continued to love them. The men who stole from her and she continued to give. The men who beat her and she continued to choose them over me. I thought there was no way she could teach me how to have confidence or to be better person.

I felt frustrated with everything that was happening to my life. I wanted a healthy mom and the perfect life. I couldn't begin to tell you how many times I cried myself to sleep. How many times I couldn't see how things could ever change. My fear was that I was going to go through the same struggle that she did.

Are you still holding on to your mother not having the right tools or the capacity to love you whole? Are you holding on to the pain and the hurt she went through? Will you forgive your mother and move forward?

I pray that you bring this hurt to an end. Stop carrying this hurt around. Ask God to heal your heart and release you from things you have no control over. God sees the situations both of you are in. He doesn't dismiss what you have gone through or what your mother didn't give herself. God is ready to restore the both of you.

God won't put anything on you that you can't bear. You will be able to make it through good times and bad times. There were some good times I shared with my mother, and I am grateful for them. I ask you to look past what your mother couldn't give you. You made it through. Instead, know that God is still a deliverer. He was and is there for you. He can still bring your mother out of situations that the enemy has planned for her. She is God's daughter too. Won't He do it!

She Stayed on Her Knees Praying

Psalms 37:23 — "One generation shall praise your works to another, and shall declare your mighty acts."

Sometimes I would walk into my mother's room and catch her praying. I thought God must know my mother directly because she was in conversation with Him morning, noon, and night. If anything came out of her mouth, you better believe God was the ending to that story. I can hear her say, "Thank you, Lord, for getting us on home safe." or "If it's His will, I will talk to you tomorrow." I would think really, Mom, you are too much. It's just the next day.

But oh, it does make my soul happy to repeat those words to my daughter now. I didn't understand that God was my mother's peace and joy. He was the rock that kept her upright.

When I was growing up, I had no clue why my mother stayed on her knees praying. I didn't see the benefits or reasons behind it. I just knew this was her daily routine, and it did not happen a day late. At that age, I didn't see the dangers or hardship of raising kids on your own, paying bills by yourself, and just trying to keep your head above water. And if that is not enough, trying to teach yourself how to be a mother. Every day there was some type of problem in the home or some child had issues. She was coming and going in all directions.

But God was willing to meet her in all those situations. She was strong and powerful and stood less than 5 feet tall. Her words were even more powerful when she talk-ed about her Father. She would sing old hymns in the morning while cooking. To this day, prayers, her old prayers, are still covering me: car wrecks, abusive rela-tionships, and drugs that were made from the enemy's hands. I took a step, and the devil took a step. It was not enough to take my mother out by broken men and unhealthy family matters; he wanted another of God's daughters too. But guess who stayed on her knees praying for her daughter? Yes, my mother, the one and only who knows how to praise her Father in the midst of the storm. My mother who has faith like Noah. She warns off the devil directly. And the days when she has no strength, she still gives God glory. I have learned not to remember her faults or her downfall, but to remember the woman who led me to my Eternal Father. She is the woman who stays on her knees praying. I love you more than life, Lilly Mae!

Chapter 6

Don't Get Sidetracked

Colossians 3:2 — "Set your minds on things above,
not on earthly things."

You Have His Identity, Not the World's

There's nothing that saddens me more in my spirit than to see my sisters and our daughters believe in the world's identity that will only turn around to change them again and again, a world that will have them focus more on the outer self than on what is inside them. A world that will teach them to master things that will last for a minute rather than what's going to keep them for a lifetime. And instead of focusing on their uniqueness, they tend to copy someone else's life. Ultimately, the true plan the enemy has in place is to make them not know who they really are.

Everything in the world—the lust of the flesh, the lust of the eyes, and the pride of life—comes not from the Father but from the world. These things all put space between you and God. They make you think you are fully aware of where they are leading you. The enjoyment they deliver lets you think that you are winning and gaining favor. But the world doesn't teach you that once it leaves the flesh, you are left empty and broken. You don't even realize this behavior has turned into your life. You search for your identity in different people, things, and places. Or you make adjustments or cut corners to find the quickest way to please your flesh. In the end, you grow to love things that are a part of brokenness and that are never meant to be a part your wholeness.

Why would you choose to love something that doesn't produce good fruit? You will hunger again. I have learned that no matter what route you take, if it doesn't lead to God's path, you will keep redefining your identity. Your heart will still jump from place to place. God has no fulfillment if His daughters do not gain peace.

Allow me to tell you that your Father has claimed you since day one. You are not lost in this crazy world; the world cannot have you. He is responsible for you. He said, I KNOW THE PLANS I HAVE FOR YOU! He desires for you to seek Him and learn His ways. He doesn't want you to learn the tricks of the enemy or fall for the scams the enemy plots. The body you are trying to have, the material things you are gaining, the ungodly relationships that come for different seasons are all temporary things. All these things on earth are fleeting. The world blindsides you by wanting you to react the way it wants you to and change when it changes. You begin telling lies to yourself and others with no remorse. Oh and then you wonder why negative things come into your life and why your emotions are out of whack. Everything you do to keep up with this world comes with a price. You will be paying back for years something that is worth nothing. He tells us over and over He will be the One who will outlast them all. Just remember the world's identity will have you chasing it for life; but it does not give life, and it will never give you rest. No matter how glamorous this world looks to you, you should take no heed to it.

Why would a powerful, intelligent daughter of God choose to be a part of something that doesn't put her in a position to be a powerful weapon for God? God is still tugging on His daughters to wake us up. He didn't intend for us to fall behind. We choose to see if the grass is greener in the world. Believe me! The grass is not green at all. The world tries to hide what God is revealing to us—that He is the Truth and the Way. He is the only One who can make us whole. Man or woman cannot make us whole. We are missing the manifest presence of God in our lives because our minds are set on things that do not matter. Do you know God has no control over you if you let this world lead you? He can no longer give you instructions on how to handle life or give you insight about who you are. God wants you to be eyes and ears for Him on earth. He is waiting for you to help Him bring down strongholds and heal the sick. Your power and influence come only through Him. Who do you think created this world?

My prayer for you is to let God show you what you're worshipping. What things or people are you placing before Him? What material things lay claim to you? There is nothing in this world that can set you free but Him. There is a dying creation that needs your help. And the only way to help your Father is to let go of this world that is not your true home.

• Awareness Questions •

Are you chasing after something that will make you forget who created you?

Are you more committed to the world and its priorities than to God?

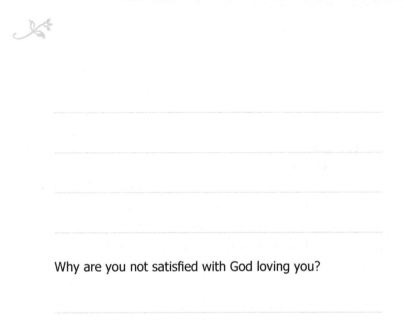

Why are you not satisfied with God loving you?

Who Needs a Mentor

Psalms 32:8 — "I will instruct you and teach you
in the way which you should go; I will counsel you
with my eye upon you."

When I first moved to Raleigh, NC, I kept hearing
the word mentor. I didn't quite understand why

having a mentor was such a big deal. I wasn't trying to start a business or go higher in my career at the time, so I didn't understand about mentors. But the word mentor was passed along at every women's event I attended, and I wanted to feel important just like everyone else. I was excited about this new idea. My goal was to get a mentor of my own as quickly as possible so I could start learning what direction I needed to take.

I began to meet women, and I would ask them if they would be my mentor, not knowing I needed to have some type of direction already in mind or even understanding that a mentor and I needed to have a great connection to sustain the mentoring process. I was amazed at the intelligent women and men I was running into. I would put them on a pedestal and speak highly of them to everyone I knew. I struggled for months trying to find the right woman mentor for me. At least I was bold enough to ask someone to mentor me. I would start the process but somehow the relationship would drift off, or I would start something new and have to change mentors. The mentors I approached couldn't quite figure out how to mentor me. I thought to myself that this mentoring stuff was a complete hot mess. Eventually, I became drained just trying to find the right someone to help me. I even thought I was foolish for trying to find a mentor for myself.

Can we look at the word mentor together? A mentor is an experienced and trusted advisor, also known as a counselor, guru, or consultant. It is a relationship in which a more experienced or more knowledgeable person helps guide a less experienced or less knowledgeable person. A mentor is someone who influences a person and helps them along their path. The mentor is there to provide guidance for what can be major decisions in life and work. And last but not least, mentoring is a process that always involves communication. I think you get the picture of where I am going with this.

How wonderful and amazing that God offers all those things. Even better, you don't have to explain who you are to Him. He knows everything in your heart. I remember in a sermon one Sunday my pastor said we all needed to go in hiding "like a turtle up under its shell." He said we were not ready to be exposed to the world. I knew He was talking directly to me. Back then, I couldn't even decide which way I was going, and I was always changing my mind. It became a full circle for me because when I would be running at the lake, I would see turtles sitting on a log. I would think, *Lord Jesus, is it still not time for me to come out from my shell?* In my mind I could see a big "NO" (yes, in capital letters). God knows us personally. He knows how we eat and how we digest. He knows our blind spots. He knows everything. I listened to God telling me that I wasn't ready, and I knew my Father knew best.

You see, the problem was that I never asked my Father to be my mentor. I was so ready to jump out there to hear other people's opinions and voices but not ready to hear what the most important voice had to say to me. I am not saying God doesn't place people in your life to guide you. There are people all around you to learn from. God just wants to know that He comes first with you. Remember, He is a jealous God. He cares about who influences His daughters. He has strategically designed your path just as a mentor would do for you.

So maybe it's time to stop asking for a mentor if you haven't even met the real mentor. God is not so far from you that He can't hear you or understand what needs to happen in your life for you to get to the next step. Psalm 94:9 says, "He who planted the ear, does He not hear? He who formed the eye, does He not see?" This is one of my favorite verses in the Bible. It calms my spirit when I read it because in that moment, I remember that God knows exactly what is going on in my life.

He longs to share with you. He has the little details to help you be a better employee, mother, sister, daughter, friend, or student. He gives you discernment and wisdom on things you would have never received from another mentor. If He hasn't given you a mentor yet, I encourage you to trust that the Lord has things lined up just for you. Even when you don't realize it, God is always teaching you where He has planted you.

• Awareness Questions •

Am I making God a priority to guide me in life?

What is something I desire in my life today that I can turn over to God?

How would I like God to help me in this?

What specific things would be helpful to me right now?

Chapter 7

For Such a Time as This

Proverbs 31:10 — "She is far more precious than jewels
and her value is far above rubies..."

Loads of Laundry

Even though I live alone now, I can't tell you that my
loads of laundry have decreased. You would think
that I still had a child in my home. Every couple of days
I know it's time to put on my laundry cap. It almost
feels like a ton of weight is on my shoulders when it's
to time wash clothes. I seem to drag the weight around
with me from the time I wash laundry until the time I
dry and fold everything. I wish I could tell you how to
make this burden go away, but I can't. Your clothes will
be there for you to wash until you are gone from this
earth.

As broken women, we know there are other loads we
carry around. We have a tendency to hold on to un-

answered questions, bitterness, and shame. And, if we let our mind wander, it can go miles down the wrong highway. Sometimes, we even let ourselves add to or subtract from what really happened. Please stop playing such negative thoughts in your mind. This will never bring you closer to the successes God has planned for you. You have to decide that His plans really do cover all of your situations. Give God the loads you are carrying. He will help you.

If you believe God is going to lead you, you need to have a new realization. You have to think your highest thoughts, thoughts so high that not even you can snatch them down. It is time to put in some work, ladies. As a woman of God, I serve the new me. I invest in the new me. I bring love to the new me. All these positive thoughts will contribute to what God has for me. Your new thoughts will become your new actions. And God is waiting for you to bring them into alignment with His. This requires you to determine what is best for you and what is going to bring you wholeness. You can only have success if you show up and do the work. My prayer to God is to bring me into His order. I need for Him to speak over my life. I am telling you this because there is territory with your name all over it. Go get it!

I want you to help your Father move you to your present. You and God can do it together! Remember, you must take action too. Here are five things to think about:

- Admit that you can't do this alone.

    Your first action is to admit that you are not strong enough to fight this battle on your own. God does not intend for you to do it alone. He knows that you are weak and not perfect. In 2 Corinthians 12:9, Paul says, "But He said to me, 'My grace is sufficient for you, for my power is made perfect in weakness.'"

- Seek counsel.

    There are people here to help you. You have to take the next step to move in that direction. They are here to give you guidance and empower you to see things in new ways. Your action plan needs strategic moves.

- Have godly friends.

    You need godly friends to hold you accountable. They will help you stay in your present. You are not here to carry this pain by yourself. The best thing about godly friends is that they will help you pray bad things away.

- Do not revert back to your past.

    Philippians 3:13 says, "Brothers, I do not consider myself yet to have taken hold of it. But one thing I do: forgetting what lies behind and straining forward to what lies ahead, I press on." When things become difficult or you don't see success happening, do not go back to your old habits. The new you and old you cannot share the same space—trying to do so will create conflict after conflict. The enemy's plan is to have you think your past is going to travel right along with you. I am here to tell you to shut down those negative thoughts immediately.

- Hold self-awareness.
  Be aware of everything you are feeling. Understand your own needs, desires, failings, habits, and everything that makes you tick. The more self-aware you become, the better you will know how deal with yourself in good times and hard times.

He Can Still Use You

Esther 4:14 — "For if you remain silent at this time, relief and deliverance for the Jews will arise from another place, but you and your father's family will perish. And who knows but that you have come into your royal position for such a time as this?"

Daughters of God, how much more does God need to prove to you that He knows every detail about your life? He sees and hears every situation you have gone through. There is nothing under the SON that you can hide from Him. I can't hide how many times I have lied to myself and others or what still hurts me to this day. Who do you think helped you get out of that abusive relationship or whose heart did He have to tug on to send you that person who kept you from something that might harm you down the road? He always walks daily by your side to protect and guide you—even when you do not ask Him to. That is His job as a Father. You can't take that away from Him. I can tell you from my own experience that He can still use you, mistakes and all. Yes, I have made mistakes. Yes, I have done things my way. Yes, I have feared what this world thinks about me. But God continues to shape me to be a better person. He encourages me so that I can start over again. I can have a future that doesn't look like my past. You can too.

I have faith that God is completing a good work in you. Every attack the enemy has set up is thrown back into the pits of hell. The enemy no longer has a right to you. The devil can't manipulate your mind into thinking you are less than you are because you didn't have a father to validate you. The enemy is no longer allowed to keep you in bondage or fear because of your upbringing. God has placed a seal on you. Our Father knitted you together while you were in your mother's womb. He knows your limitations and deficiencies. He set these things to make you depend on Him. All healing and deliverance come from Him. Please remember, Sis, He will always be your good stronghold or strong tower. Your main goal is to press forward and continue to grow in Him.

I beg you to please forgive yourself for the things that the enemy disguised. Forgive yourself for thinking you couldn't be used for such a time as this. A good thing about your Father is that you don't have to hide any-thing from God or be embarrassed. He sympathizes with your deepest pain. You have been rejected, abused, and discounted for so long. You may even think God doesn't see you doing great things. God does see you! And I see you too!

Your time is coming! I want you to start believing in yourself and believe that God is working on your be-half. You think you have to stay in that same place or with the same people. This is so not true. Even our Father does not stay in the same place. He is always moving around trying to find someone to FOLLOW Him and GO HIGHER IN HIM. Promotions come from Him. Not man. Not a job. Not material things.

Through every situation, God is leading you more from the world and closer to Him. He knows what is needed to help you understand that you are worth more than rubies and gold. He has pushed and pulled you out of places that you don't belong. When you finally make a decision to surrender, He will start to do your ground-work. I have learned that He uses people and situations to develop your character so that you can be used for His glory. He has convicted you to forgive people and love them even more. As for me, not only am I chang-ing my ways to please Him, I will continue to go higher in Christ.

Have you heard the story of Esther in the Bible? Esther

has become one of my favorite books. Esther was an orphan raised by her cousin, Mordecai. Her name, Hadassah, was changed to Esther to hide her Hebrew heritage so that she would have a chance at something bigger than her heritage permitted. Esther went through twelve months of beauty treatments—six months with oil of myrrh and six months with perfumes and preparations for beautifying her—all to be presented to the king of the land. She was chosen by the king. The king loved Esther more than all the women in the court, and she found favor and kindness with Him. Esther learned how to be brave and how to set standards. She became skillful at influencing people. Her cousin knew that she was put in place by God for something important, but Esther had to realize that for herself. Esther's brave actions saved the nation of Israel from being destroyed. She was considered bold and courageous by her people then and still is honored today.

The challenge is right in front of you. Do you want to be used by God? If so, get ready for your awakening. Esther had a teachable and humble spirit. She lived a very different life than she was born into. No doubt she wanted to give up on the new life at times when so much was expected of her. But God spoke over her life, and she kept moving forward.

This process didn't happen overnight for Esther, and it won't for you either. Your Father wants to do the same thing with you, but first God has to purge out all the ugly stuff you have inside of you that you've held on to. Your spirit has to be aligned with what God wants you for. He does not want you to go back and forth between your old life and your new life or question if you are the right person for the job He is calling you to do. You are always going to fall short of His Glory. We all are!

In time, you will embrace the new you wholeheartedly. He wants you to see a side of you that elevates you to the royal status of His beloved daughter. Think about the awesome things He can do through you. As you grow and evolve, life begins to welcome the new you. Life has to obey what God calls forth in you. You need to believe with me that God can use you. God wants to use you. And God knows how to use you. I am so excited for you!

I wanted to share the story of Esther because it applies to you and me. It helps us understand that we are chosen daughters. We have to see that God gives us resources and people to help accomplish our goals. He lines up things for us so we will be noticed at the right time. We don't have to fit in or be a part of this world to be noticed. Esther was unknown until her cousin Mordecai, following God's plan, helped her get noticed by the king and be raised to a position of influence. Your Father sees you doing right things and will reward you in His time. When you get a chance, please read the Esther story in the Old Testament for yourself.

Lord God Almighty, great is Your faithful name. You are Lord of all lords, Kings of all kings. I praise You today because no matter how far we think we are away from You, You have us in the palm of Your hand. Lord, I pray for those who feel defeated and unworthy. I pray for those who do not know their true place in life. I lift up those who have never heard what they are really worth, those still searching for validation. Lord, they need to hear Your truth. God, you know their names and the number of hairs on their heads. Keep them close to You, Lord, like a mother would her infant.

Show them that you are the God who makes a way out of no way. Let them know You can use them. Give them hope to carry on each day. Use Your powerful word to fight off lies that bombard them daily. Help them see who they are through Your wonderful eyes. Hug them, Jesus. Give them songs to sing so they will feel close to You. In the mighty name above all names, Jesus, I pray. Amen

Chapter 8

Turn Around and Give God the Glory

Psalms 68:11 — "The lord gives the word; the women who announce the news are a mighty throng."

You and God Are a Perfect Match

This is the chapter where you will bring everything back to God. It is where you will look back and see all the moving pieces. You will see it was always you and Him in this together. I do this on a daily basis. How does a lost woman come to know someone who will challenge her life forever? Know a God who will have her search no longer? Find the water that will have her thirst no more? No man will ever compare to this love your Father gives you!

I remember when I was confronted by God. He was so amazing and powerful! It was the moment that redirected the course of my life. I truly believe that God knows when we are finally ready to meet Him. He knows that the world has nothing lasting to offer us. He meets us at the well to have a One-on-one encounter. Despite our foolishness and ignorance toward Him, He reveals to us who He is and why we are going to serve Him! I can just stay right there and cry out to Him.

This is the time to be vulnerable with Him, not guarded. He already knows every path you have taken and every crazy act you have done. Your Father understands how you have struggled looking for love in all the wrong places. It is no surprise to Him. Sis, for years I searched for a man or people to fill voids in my life that only God could fill. My heart was broken over and over trying to figure how I could make things better or to make that person see I could love them more than the next person could. The lies you tell yourself! Please stop! I didn't know the One I was searching for was already in my heart. He was waiting for me to know it. I encourage you to open your heart when He meets you at that place. It is coming! Then make sure you run and tell everyone who He is. Don't keep this a secret. What a love story it is—just waiting to happen.

He Deserves It

Luke 13:13 — "Then he put his hands on her, and immediately she straightened up and praised God."

I never knew one encounter with God would have me praising His name for the rest of my life. It is that simple. It was His touch that would bring healing in my life. When God calls you out from confusion and separates you from darkness, you see things more clearly. No longer will you chase after people and things that only cause you to repeat the same past behavior. People want to make you glorify them instead of God. No one in this world is comparable to your Father. How can you sit back and shut your heart and mouth to a Father who protects you from harm, covers your children, and delivers your soul from hell?

Our desire should be to focus on Him and give Him the glory at all times. I have learned at every opportunity to praise Him. I do it with boldness and courage. I am not ashamed of His name. I praise him whether I am in the car, on my job—anywhere. We have to be ready and willing to let people know who changed us. I desire to be obedient to my father's voice. Read 1 Peter 3:15. It says, "But in your hearts revere Christ as Lord. Always be prepared to give an answer to everyone who asks you to give the reason for the hope that you have. But do it with gentleness and respect." It is imperative for others to see how we lift up His name.

What person do you know who has always been consistent and trustworthy on every occasion throughout your life, even when you turn away? We fall short to God's will and word many times. And still he waits for us to come back and receives us with open arms.

God has given me more than I expected. My life has turned for the better. I am a new creature in Him. All the old things have passed away. I am grateful to say I do not look like my past. He let me start over. And that was the best part! Now my happiness comes from Him, not from other people. He shows me that I have authority and influence in this world. He challenges me to be a better mother, daughter, employee, and friend. My confidence is building daily. I have accomplished goals through His strength and wisdom. He downloads secrets into my spirit. These are things I can't learn from this world. They come only when I spend time with Him. He only wants the best for me. I was willing to surrender to Him. My hope was to give him all of me. To let this change come about, I asked the Holy Spirit to help me with this process. The good news is that God wants to do the same thing for you!

God is willing to raise the bar in your life if you let Him. He brings people into your life to turn up the heat. He slowly takes you through different stages to purge out all the ugly things that came into your life without His approval. Then He gives you your own sweet smelling perfume to change the world around you. Can you imagine becoming this powerful woman of God who brings other chosen sisters to Him to help Him do His work? Well, know that you have been kept for such a time as this. Sis, your goal now is to pursue Jesus and find out what His plan is for your new life. He deserves it and so do you!

Dancing with Your Father

Luke 1:46 — "And Mary said: "My soul glorifies the Lord..."

There is nothing more beautiful than a daughter who has the chance to dance with her Father. I never had the opportunity to dance with my father. But if I had, I know that moment would have been perfect for me. I imagine looking into his eyes and wanting him to validate everything about me. If you have these thoughts too, remember this: when God formed you in your mother's womb, He knew you would miss out on occasions like this. He knew that you would need more love, more validation, and more understanding from Him. It is in Him we will find confirmation of who we are. God does not want you to miss a beat from your life. He desires you to dance with Him anytime you feel like dancing with your father.

I want to help you connect with your Eternal Father so I have listed four ways you can dance with Him:

Stay Connected — Submission

First of all, you need a proper understanding of submission. To be submissive to God means being ready for and obedient to His authority and will. You must understand all authority comes from God, the Creator of heaven and earth, and you are commanded to submit to Him in all your ways. God wants to lead you in all His ways. You should submit to God because He desires you to be obedient. Why would you question something that holds the great purpose of your life? He has many things to show you. He destined for you to know His will. The woman who grows spiritually is the woman that God exalts. If you want to be a daughter of God, you must fall in love with His commands.

Stay Connected — Prayer

A daughter of God must know she can't bypass this one. It is how she communicates with her Father daily. It is how He communicates to her—mind, body, and soul. This is how your relationship starts with your Father. God must know you are willing to pray to Him at all times. There should be nothing that gets in the way of your prayers. Not your family. Not your friends. Not your job. When you pray, you are thirsting for His word in your life. You are showing Him you are willing to listen to anything He has to say to you. It is easy to miss out on God by underestimating the power of prayer. He wants you to come away from anything that is not pleasing to Him. If you are struggling with any kind of sin, you can seek God in prayer for His strength and wisdom in that situation. God has deliverance for you and your family in your prayers. Let Him enter in your heart and spread the good news.

Stay Connected — Faith

We live by faith, not by sight. You must understand the power of this statement in your faith walk. Sisters, having faith is what pleases God. He knows you may not see His work in you yet. He wants you to be patient. He will answer you in accordance with His will for you—and He knows best for you. He cannot move powerfully in your life until He knows you will trust in Him completely. Psalm 9:10 says, "Those who know your name trust in you, for you, Lord, have never forsaken those who seek you." God will never leave you doubtful as people often do. He is intentional about His relationship with you. He expects the same from you. He has promises over your life and is ready to deliver them to you. A woman who has faith in God will not fear anything that God puts in her path. She cannot be moved or shaken by anything that does not line up with His word. A woman of faith is confident in her Father's word. She knows that every fruitful thing she plants, her Father will bless. It takes courage to show others how to live faithfully. And not least of all, a woman of faith loves the Lord with all her heart.

Stay Connected — Time

Cherish the time you spend with your Father. This is the time that God can talk to you One-on-one. Let Him see that you are willing to slow down your day just to let Him in your heart. Sometimes life can get so busy that you do not give God time to make an impression in your heart. I wake up every morning knowing that this is the best time that I can give to Him. I never regret the time I spend with my Father. I want to give Him my best energy and focus. I am not concerned or anxious to do anything else at this time. I am willing to give Him my full attention.

Before I start, I ask Him to remove any distractions that will separate me from Him. I pray to gain His strength in that day. I also ask him to remove any bitterness, anger, or harmful motives, hidden and unhidden, from my heart. Sometimes we have hidden agendas we do not know we have inside of us. We have to seek God in everything. Your personal time is between you and God. I encourage you to be intentional about this time. You are important to Him, and He wants to talk to you every day. Remember, each moment you spend with your Father is another opportunity to become more like Him.

* * *

• Awareness Questions •

What does it mean to you to give God glory?

Are you willing to commit to giving God glory?

What are ways you can glorify Him?

What are specific ways you can stay connected to God?

_____

_____

_____

_____

_____

Do you let others know He deserves all the praise?

_____

_____

_____

_____

_____

Chapter 9

Reclaim Who You Are

2 Corinthians 5:17 — "This means that anyone who belongs to Christ has become a new person. The old life is gone; a new life has begun!"

It is no secret that many of us are fatherless daughters. We adapted to the world the best way we knew how. We learned to become independent, and we created our own paths. Our most treacherous times are experiencing setbacks, limitations, and betrayal in our lives. You and I have so many stops placed in front us by the enemy, we condition ourselves to be fearful each time we have an opportunity to move forward. Most of our best-day opportunities were stolen by people we thought would never leave us. But no matter what cards we are dealt, we choose to survive and not die. It is in this moment of choice that we can prepare to become greater. We can shift our focus to what is to become rather than dwell on what has happened in the past. This is the time to release any hatred, blame, or resentment we have toward others and ourselves, the time to claim who we were born to be as daughters of God.

I believe that you are now aware of a mighty God who can do all things for His daughters. It is up to you to be courageous in your life. You must create new experiences, start new traditions with your family, and express your love in new ways. Your intentions must be more powerful than ever before. This means showing up present in every area of life knowing that you make a difference in this world. Know that if you aren't part of the plan, people will miss out on an awesome person. The key is in knowing that you have power. God is offering that power to you so that you can give Him glory. I truly want you to live life knowing that you are not alone. God knows where you have been and knows where you are going. Trust God and get ready to claim who you are.

* * *

Here are five simple lessons I have learned about growing in faith.

1. Grow a little each day!

You set the start and stop button when it comes to growing each day. You have the power to learn as much as you desire. And no matter how far you think you are behind, God will get you on track. Everyone who knows me knows I love to learn. I want to learn everything my Father wants to teach me so I can give Him even more glory. I truly believe if you want something in life, you must become a learner.

God is giving you insight each day to rediscover who you are. He is finding the right people and right opportunities to get you where you need to be. He wants you to focus on setting yourself up for success, yours and His. You can get prepared for this by putting in practice what's true in life. Your goal is to rediscover who you are, determine what you believe in, and learn what is best for you.

By gaining knowledge, you have opportunities to see what doors can open for you. You will gain information that you would never have learned if you weren't curious. There is always something to discover each day. Seek it out and know that you can grow in every way. The better equipped you are about life and in life, the more God can use you for His glory.

2. Set boundaries

It is so vital that you learn how to set healthy boundaries. If you do not set your boundaries, you hinder your growth process. You will stay stuck in one place, still striving to please everyone except the One who counts and yourself. You will start to lose the focus of who you are and what is next to come for you on God's path. As a result, you will have conflict within yourself.

I recommend that you listen to how you feel. This

means taking time to step back and wait for the right answer to reach you. You have to be comfortable with making these decisions, nothing should be done out of fear. Also, learn how to say no to things that don't advance where you are going in life. This means sometimes needing to say no to material things, places, activities, and even certain people in your life. There may be times you have to sacrifice something you want in order to attain something much more important that you need in God's service, but know the reward will be worth the sacrifice.

You are here to serve a purpose. There should be nothing that gets in the way of that purpose. Setting boundaries teaches you self-awareness, discipline, and self-love.

3. Spend some time alone

I know this might seem scary to some of you. Being alone can help you face truth about your life. I can assure you this will be another benefit to your life. When you spend time alone, you are able to gain clarity on what God is calling you to do. He can teach you how to connect to Him and your true self.

Spending time alone allows God to download His secrets for your life and teach you things this world cannot teach you. By spending time alone, you can take time for internal reflection—check in with yourself to see how you are doing. This helps you take care of yourself and your needs.

Remember, before you can help this world, you must make sure your heart, mind, and spirit are full of God's purpose for you—so spend some of your alone time with your Father.

4. Your love matters

You are more than capable of making good decisions about love in your life. You have the power and confidence to recognize the love God has placed inside of you and to love yourself as a daughter of God. You need to understand that until you love yourself first, no one will ever see the value you bring.

Many of us are guilty of giving away too freely the love we have in us, not knowing that our ability to love is a gift from God. Do you know how deep your love runs? I suggest you look back over your life and see how far you have come. The love runs so deep it kept you going when you wanted to give up. It helped you survive the hurt and pain that could have destroyed you. It transformed darkness into light. The love you have for yourself is the love that keeps on giving you strength.

5. Be grateful forever

Gratefulness definitely should go on your priority list

every day. You have so much to be grateful for in life. Your Father has given you another chance to open your eyes and see the truth. He has given you another chance to explore life in a healthy way. You get to choose what can enhance your life and uncover gifts you never knew existed in yourself.

Take the time to see His wonders around you and within you—the rising sun, the moon hanging in the sky, the glory of our beautiful earth, and the gifts the Lord has given you. In everything give thanks to Him. Giving thanks to God keeps you in right relationship with Him and, in return, He gives you the peace you need daily. Here's to the new best part of your second life!

* * *

Please pray this prayer with me:

Lord, I recognize that I have not lived my life according to Your ways. I have been leaning on my own understanding. I need You in my life; I want You in my life. No longer will I close my heart to You. I am ready to trust You as my Lord and Savior. I believe You are the Son of God who died on the cross for my sins and rose from the dead on the third day. Thank you for giving me eternal life. Come into my heart, Lord Jesus, and be my savior. Please send your Holy Spirit to help me obey You and do Your will for the rest of my life. In your holy name I pray. Amen

Here are eleven things that have helped me learn how to be a daughter to God, my Father. I hope you find them helpful in your journey.

1. Commit to making God your PRIORITY.

2. Ask God to reveal to you the times He was there in your life. This way you will know He has been there the whole time without you begging or asking Him.

3. Accept that God knows everything about your past. He is not looking at you and thinking you are worthless and can't be loved by Him. As a matter of fact, He wants to be there to clean you up.

4. Understand that God knew you before you were born. Remember that you were no surprise to Him. He had you in His plan from the beginning.

5. Study His word so that you will have a better understanding of your Father.

6. Spend time with Him silently so that you can hear His truth.

7. Let go of any anger or blame you want to place on your earthly father. God was always in place to protect and guide you.

8. Trust in Him that He has everything worked out for your

good. You don't have to chase anybody down or worry about how things will work out. God will either open the door or close the door in accordance with His will. He will not give you more than you can bear. He knows when the timing is right for what He has in mind for you.

9. Give God the glory always and in all ways. It pleases Him to know you find Him worthy to be praised. I always believe it makes Him smile.

10. Understand that no one can fill that void in you but God. He is the only One who will not have you thirst again when you drink the water of life!

11. Embrace that HE CHOSE YOU!

* * *

Please help me share with our sisters that we are committed to helping this message come true for them!

Here's how I am committed to my sisters:

- I am committed to teaching my sisters how to make God a priority in their lives.

- I am committed to helping my sisters understand their Father loves them.

- I am committed to helping my sisters build their faith.

- I am committed to encouraging my sisters to understand they can be used for God's purposes.

- I am committed to praying for my sisters.

- I am committed to sharing hope with my sisters.

- I am committed to taking my sisters higher in God.

- I am committed to moving my sisters into places of influence.

- I am committed to helping my sisters spread the word about Christ.

My prayer is that each and every one of you will receive God as your Father. Give Him the opportunity to be a part of your everyday life. Let Him know that you are willing to move forward and not look back on your past. Know that He has been there in your life the whole time. He did not leave you lonely and uncovered. He called on you before you were in your mother's womb. He chose you to be His daughter. How amazing is this? You are a daughter of a King! He is so ready to show you how much He cares and loves you. Trust Him with your life completely. I promise you, you were never fatherless.

My hope is to see you prosper in life. You deserve it!

You are the apple of His eye!

Thank You

Thank you for reading this book. I hope the message spoke to your heart, lifted your spirits, and made you hungry for more time with your Father. The goal of living in the light and love of Father God is to shape ourselves for healthy relationships with our own "self" and with others and to know we have value as His "Chosen Daughters."

I would truly appreciate your help in sharing this message. If the message touched you, would you please take a few minutes and leave a review for this book on Amazon.com? I would be so grateful for your thoughts.

Respectfully,
Carmen McLean

About the Author

Throughout her life, Carmen S. McLean has always had a passion to encourage women and see them grow into their full potential. As a Certified Life Coach, her desire is to guide women to claim their role as chosen daughters just as she has.

As she continues to overcome life's hurdles and challenges, she grows ever closer to her Heavenly Father and is stronger day by day. In the sharing of her experiences, Carmen teaches others to press forward to become whole and influential women in their own lives.

Carmen is a daughter of a praying woman and a single mother of a beautiful daughter.

Made in the USA
Las Vegas, NV
20 December 2024

14999267R00059